NASHVILLE PREDATORS

BY LUKE HANLON

Book design by Maggie Villaume
Cover design by Maggie Villaume

Photographs ©: Mark Humphrey/AP Images, cover, 4–5, 8, 13, 15, 19, 24–25; Peter Joneleit/Cal Sport Media/AP Images, 7; Elise Amendola/AP Images, 10–11; Frederick Breedon/AP Images, 16–17; Chris Carlson/AP Images, 20; Kathy Willens/AP Images, 23; Steve Roberts/Cal Sport Media/ZUMA Wire/AP Images, 27; Andy Clayton-King/AP Images, 28

Press Box Books, an imprint of Press Room Editions.

ISBN
978-1-63494-676-6 (library bound)
978-1-63494-700-8 (paperback)
978-1-63494-746-6 (epub)
978-1-63494-724-4 (hosted ebook)

Library of Congress Control Number: 2022919281

Distributed by North Star Editions, Inc.
2297 Waters Drive
Mendota Heights, MN 55120
www.northstareditions.com

Printed in the United States of America
Mankato, MN
082023

ABOUT THE AUTHOR

Luke Hanlon is a sportswriter and editor based in Minneapolis.

TABLE OF CONTENTS

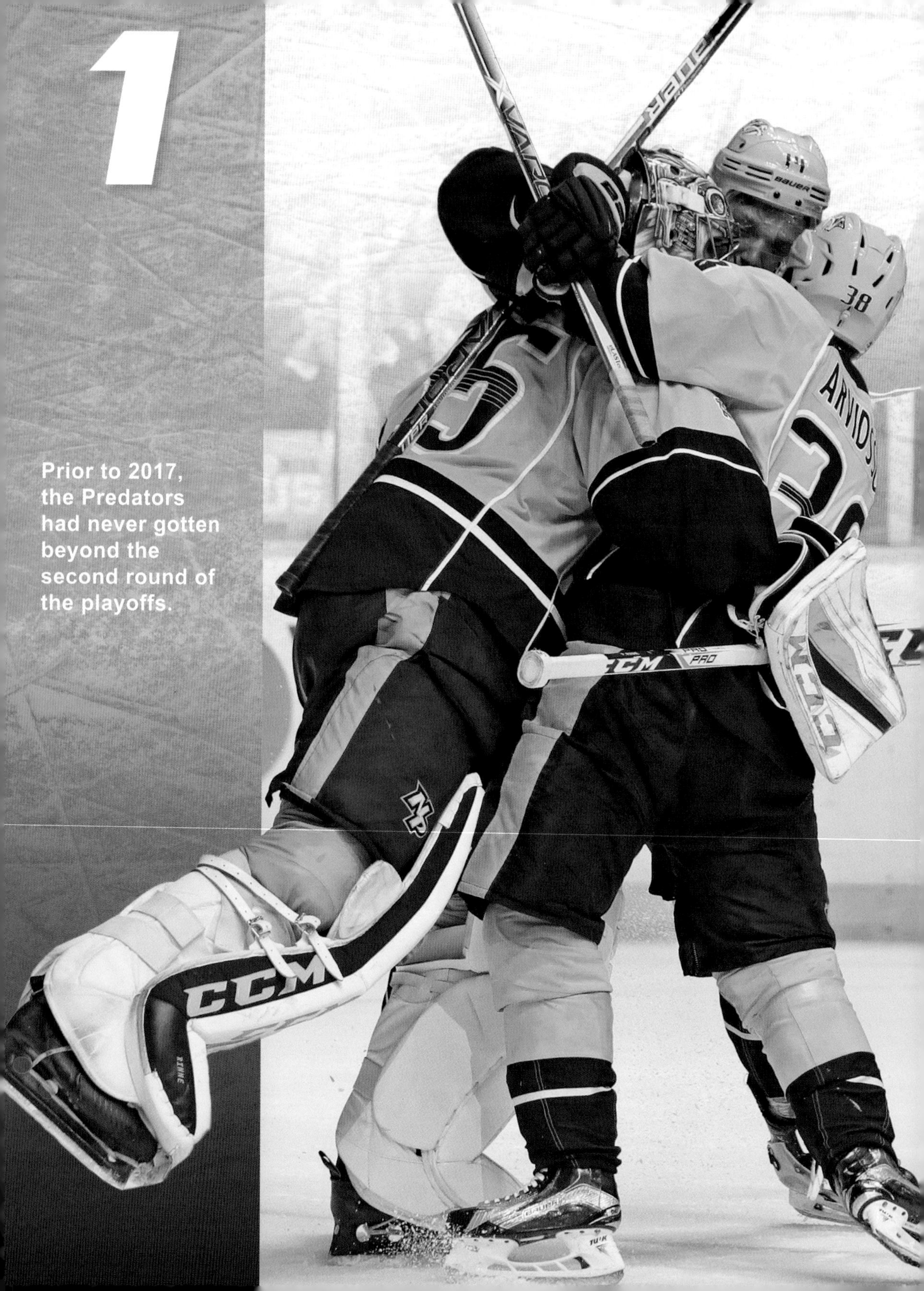

1

Prior to 2017, the Predators had never gotten beyond the second round of the playoffs.

HAT TRICK *HERO*

The Nashville Predators creeped into the 2017 National Hockey League (NHL) postseason. No playoff team had fewer points in the regular season than Nashville. But the Predators turned it on in the playoffs. They swept the favored Chicago Blackhawks in the first round. They then beat the St. Louis Blues in six games. For the first time in the

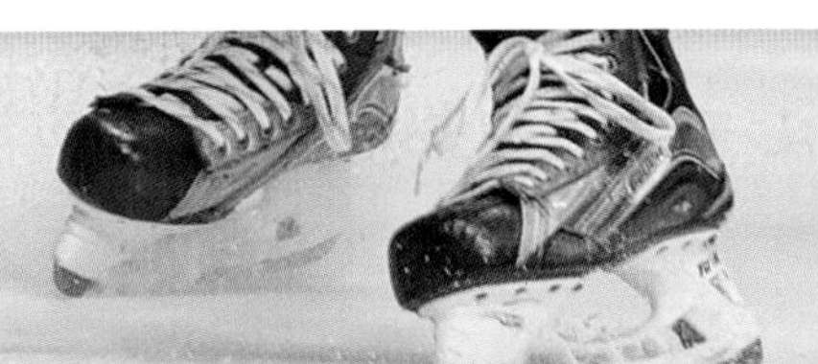

team's 18 seasons, Nashville was in the conference finals.

The Anaheim Ducks awaited. The two teams split the first four games. The Predators then won Game 5 on the road. This gave them a 3–2 series lead. The Stanley Cup Final was one win away.

More than 17,000 energetic fans packed Nashville's Bridgestone Arena for Game 6. Predators center Colton Sissons scored his second goal of the game early in the third period to put Nashville up 3–1. But the Ducks fought back. They tied the game with just over 11 minutes left. Nashville needed someone to step up.

The Predators were attacking with just over six minutes left. Sissons carried

Nashville's Austin Watson (left) and Mattias Ekholm (right) celebrate a goal in Game 1 against the Ducks.

the puck into the offensive zone. Two Anaheim defenders stopped him. The puck popped free. Nashville forward Calle Jarnkrok took control. Then he

Colton Sissons (right) celebrates his third goal of Game 6 against the Ducks with Calle Jarnkrok.

sent a pass across the ice. Sissons was wide open. The center shot a one-timer. Ducks goalie Jonathan Bernier had no chance. Sissons's teammates swarmed him in celebration. His hat trick put them within minutes of a trip to the Stanley Cup Final. It was only the second three-goal performance in Predators playoff history. The Nashville crowd erupted.

The Predators scored two empty-net goals to win 6–3. They were on to the Stanley Cup Final for the first time.

UNLIKELY STAR

The 2016–17 season was Colton Sissons's third in the NHL. In 109 career games, he had scored 13 goals. He scored six during the 2017 playoff run.

2

The Predators celebrate a third-period winner in a 1999 game.

SMASHVILLE'S START

Nashville, Tennessee, was ready for a hockey team before the Predators started playing. The city opened Nashville Arena in 1996. The NHL offered Nashville a team in 1997. But there was a catch. The team's owners needed to sell 12,000 season tickets in order to join the NHL.

Nashville didn't have a hockey tradition to sell fans on. But the city does have a musical history.

Ownership decided to lean on that instead. The team put up billboards featuring musicians like Garth Brooks. The plan worked. Nashville was invited to join the NHL for the 1998–99 season.

The Predators chose center David Legwand as their first draft pick in 1998. He would go on to play in Nashville for 15 seasons. Those early seasons did not go well, however. The Predators finished last in their division in 1998–99.

BECOMING THE PREDATORS

In 1971, scientists discovered bones of a saber-toothed tiger in what is now downtown Nashville. That discovery inspired the team's name. First, the team introduced a logo featuring a saber-toothed tiger. Then a vote was held to pick a name. Predators won the vote.

David Legwand tallied 566 points over 15 seasons in Nashville.

After four years of losing, fans became frustrated. The team still never made the playoffs. Attendance dropped by more than 1,000 fans per game. The owners decided a new slogan chosen by the fans would give the team an identity. One stood out more than any other. That's how "Smashville" was born in 2002.

Smashville combined the physical play of hockey with the hits of country music. The team wanted games at the arena to be a party. But attendance still dropped. And the play on the ice continued to decline too.

That started to change in 2003–04. Legwand and winger Scott Walker led the Predators to the playoffs for the first time. They met the Detroit Red Wings in the first round. Detroit had won the Stanley Cup just two years before. The underdog Predators won their first two home games.

The Predators celebrate a goal in their first-ever playoff win in 2004.

This tied the series 2–2. The Red Wings went on to win the series. But Smashville was gaining confidence.

3

Shea Weber played 763 games over 11 seasons in Nashville.

STALKING *PREY*

Ryan Suter and Shea Weber were both ready for the NHL by the 2005–06 season. The Predators had drafted the two defensemen in 2003. They were still young when they arrived in Nashville. But they proved to be one of the best defensive partnerships in the league.

That same season, the Predators also added more experience. They signed forward

Paul Kariya. The future Hall of Famer scored 31 goals in 2005–06. That was the most in a season in team history. Kariya played in Nashville for two seasons. And he led the team in points both years. The Predators made the playoffs in those seasons. But they lost in the first round each time.

Nashville finally broke through in the 2011 playoffs. The Predators played the Anaheim Ducks in the first round. The series was tied 2–2 before Game 5

SLAPSHOT SHEA

Shea Weber had a powerful shot. That made him a must-see competitor in the NHL Hardest Shot competition at the league's annual All-Star weekend. Weber won the competition four times. His first win was in 2015. He shot the puck 108.5 miles per hour (174.6 kmh).

Paul Kariya was a force offensively. He averaged 0.98 points per game while with the Predators.

in Anaheim. The Predators were behind 3–2 with under a minute left. Then Weber stepped up. The team captain ripped a perfect shot from the blue line. The goal

Jerred Smithson celebrates his game-winning goal in the 2011 playoffs.

sent Weber's teammates into a frenzy. Center Jerred Smithson then scored in overtime to give Nashville the series lead. The Predators then won Game 6 at home. It was their first playoff series win.

The playoff run stopped there, however. The Vancouver Canucks knocked the Predators out in the second round. The Predators lost again in the second round to the Phoenix Coyotes in 2012. Then Nashville missed the playoffs the following two seasons.

The Predators still had plenty of talent. Weber was one of the best defensemen in the league. And Roman Josi and Seth Jones were talented up-and-comers. General manager David Poile and head coach Barry Trotz had been there since the team's start in 1998. But Poile fired Trotz in 2014, hoping a fresh face behind the bench could get the team winning again.

PEKKA RINNE

The Predators selected Pekka Rinne in the 2004 draft. Not much was expected from the Finnish goalie. But he became one of the best players in team history.

Rinne was a monster in goal. His huge body gave up little room in front of goal for opposing players. He used that size to lead the NHL in saves in 2011–12. Rinne also led the league in shutouts twice. One of those seasons was 2017–18. He was so good that year that he won the Vezina Trophy. That is given to the best goaltender in the NHL each season.

Rinne retired from the NHL after the 2020–21 season. He had played his entire 15-year career in Nashville. The Predators retired his No. 35 jersey the following year. Rinne became the first player in team history to have his number retired.

Pekka Rinne registered
60 shutouts while in Nashville.

4

Filip Forsberg broke the Predators' career goals record in 2022.

STILL HUNTING

Nashville hired Peter Laviolette as head coach before the 2014–15 season. By then, promising young center Filip Forsberg was ready for his first full NHL season. Defenseman Roman Josi was becoming a star alongside Shea Weber. And Pekka Rinne was one of the best goalies in the league.

That core brought the Predators back to the playoffs in 2015. A year later the Predators beat the Anaheim Ducks in the first round of the playoffs. But they fell to the San Jose Sharks in the next round.

That offseason, the Predators and the Montreal Canadiens swapped superstar defensemen. Weber went to Montreal. P. K. Subban came to Nashville. It was a bold move. Weber had become a fan favorite in Nashville. But it didn't take long for Predators fans to love Subban. He helped Nashville make a run to the Stanley Cup Final in his first year with the team.

The Predators won their first two home games in the Final. That tied the series 2–2. But the defending champion

P. K. Subban recorded a team-high 43 assists in 2017–18.

Pittsburgh Penguins shut out Nashville the next two games to win the Cup.

The Predators bounced back in 2017–18. It was actually the best regular

Roman Josi's 72 assists in 2021–22 were the best in a single season in team history.

season in team history. Nashville won the Presidents' Trophy for the first time. That is awarded to the team with the most points in the regular season. But the Predators didn't make it back to the Stanley Cup Final. They lost in the second round to the Winnipeg Jets.

Playoff woes continued for the next four seasons. The Predators never made it past the first round. But the team still had stars like Forsberg and Josi. A solid core remained in Smashville. And the fans had hope the team could deliver a championship.

OUTDOOR HOCKEY

The NHL held its first outdoor hockey game in 2003. In 2022, an outdoor game was held in Nashville for the first time. The game was held at Nissan Stadium, home of the Tennessee Titans. More than 68,000 fans saw the Predators lose 3–2 to the Tampa Bay Lightning.

• NASHVILLE PREDATORS
QUICK STATS

TEAM HISTORY: Nashville Predators (1998–)

STANLEY CUP CHAMPIONSHIPS: 0

KEY COACHES:

- Barry Trotz (1998–2014): 557 wins, 479 losses, 60 ties, 100 overtime losses
- Peter Laviolette (2014–20): 248 wins, 143 losses, 60 overtime losses

HOME ARENA: Bridgestone Arena (Nashville, TN)

MOST CAREER POINTS: David Legwand (566)

MOST CAREER GOALS: Filip Forsberg (220)

MOST CAREER ASSISTS: Roman Josi (402)

MOST CAREER SHUTOUTS: Pekka Rinne (60)

**Stats are accurate through the 2021–22 season.*

GLOSSARY

BLUE LINE
The line that separates the three zones on the ice.

CAPTAIN
A team's leader.

DRAFT
An event that allows teams to choose new players coming into the league.

GENERAL MANAGER
The person in charge of a sports team, whose duties include signing and trading players.

OVERTIME
An additional period of play to decide a game's winner.

SHUTOUT
A game in which one team wins and prevents the other team from scoring.

SWEPT
When a team has won all the games in a series.

ZONE
One of three areas on a hockey rink that are separated by blue lines.

TO LEARN MORE

BOOKS

Davidson, B. Keith. *NHL*. New York: Crabtree Publishing, 2022.

Duling, Kaitlyn. *Women in Hockey*. Lake Elmo, MN: Focus Readers, 2020.

Hewson, Anthony K. *GOATs of Hockey*. Minneapolis: Abdo Publishing, 2022.

MORE INFORMATION

To learn more about the Nashville Predators, go to **pressboxbooks.com/AllAccess**.

These links are routinely monitored and updated to provide the most current information available.

INDEX